# CONFETTI DANCERS

Sue Burge is a freelance creative writing and film studies tutor and writing mentor based in North Norfolk. Her poetry has been widely published and anthologised. *Lumière* (Hedgehog Poetry Press), Sue's debut pamphlet, explores Paris's cinematic heritage. Her first collection, *In the Kingdom of Shadows,* was published by Live Canon in 2018. Her second pamphlet, *The Saltwater Diaries* (Hedgehog Poetry Press), came out in 2020. This is her second collection.

**First Published in 2021**
By Live Canon Poetry Ltd
www.livecanon.co.uk

978-1-909703-47-6

A CIP catalogue record for this book is available from the British Library.

Cover Photograph: © Jane Hobson

## To Bryce

I learn this quilt will contain
a hundred thousand unknown names

all forty-two of my facial muscles
try not to cry as I stitch the memory

of the day you showed me your arms
bejewelled with sarcoma,

how I felt the stutter of your
dancing heartbeat.

I re-imagine you flying home
to die in the Australian sun

while we mourned among
the cold grey bricks of Rotherhithe.

Then the others too were claimed,
one by one, long and slow and cruel

as purgatory. I honour your name
in thread the colour of sunlight,

whispering all the news of all the years
you never knew me.

*from 'In the Kingdom of Shadows' (2018, Live Canon)*

# Acknowledgments

'Interlude in a Locked Room' and 'Triangulation' both appeared in issues of *Modern Poetry in Translation* online, in response to Transreading projects resulting from Poetry School courses with the inspirational Elzbieta Wójcik-Leese. 'The Distractor Brides of St Petersburg' appeared in *The Literary Bohemian*, 'Russian Doll' was published in *London Grip* and 'Mother Russia' in *The Pangolin Review*. 'Taken' appeared in *Lighthouse* and 'Zone' was featured in *Words for the Wild*. 'Margot Fonteyn, 1944' is part of a prose poem sequence which appeared in *The Ekphrastic Review*.

'Read Their Lips' is the first part of a ten-poet collaborative project curated by Simon Barraclough and Julia Bird. It was performed at The Cinema Museum before a screening of *Battle of the Somme 1916*. Each poet responded to a section of the film and this was my contribution. 'Snowdream', 'Glow' and '#stayathome' all appear in the anthology *Pestilence* edited by Peter Pegnall and Gerard Noyau (Lapwing). 'Snowdream' first appeared on *WRITE Where We Are NOW*, Manchester Metropolitan University's exploration of poetry in lockdown, curated by Carol Ann Duffy. 'Glow' first appeared as part of *100 Words of Solitude's Life in the Time of Corona* showcase. 'Mother, folded small' and 'Obituary for your last pair of ballet shoes' appeared in *The Lonely Crowd*.

Thank you to my great friend and mentor Heidi Williamson for her, as always, invaluable advice on both individual poems and the whole collection; to Vanessa Lindsay, my dear friend whom I met at the Royal Academy of Dancing – our reminiscences helped to shape many of these poems; to Julia Webb for her insight and encouragement; to Jeffery Sugarman and his fantastic band of Limónistas; and finally to the Norwich Stanza group for their feedback on many of these poems.

In the early 1990s I discovered the NAMES Project (AIDS Memorial Quilt) in San Francisco where people stitch panels to memorialise those they lost in the AIDS pandemic. This quilt is referenced in the poem 'To Bryce'.

# Contents

## I

## II

## Interlude

## III

## Coda

I

# Cento

*after Alexander Ulanov – trans. by Alex Cigale & Michelle Murphy*


Florist, your bones are made of untouched night,
lime is in your dreams, snow in your hands

you are pale, barely noticeable, a lip-reader…
Time is a habit, ten to seven, the wind

all dark windows and void, a Christmas tree's shadow.
You are capable, but it is still too early to build

an igloo. Say my name in tempo, thread a twig –
come and regret our gridlocked days

futile pulse, giving back nothing in return –
       a stone, a field, a vacuum.

## Edit

a monochrome crowd in a pale plaza
onion-domed church to the right
town hall to the left
everyone moves in jerky unison as if a great back
has somehow turned away
in a cosmic game of musical statues:
two lovers on a bicycle
bickering about bread and potatoes
the kind of couple Chagall loves to show
soaring over rickety rooftops
a weary charwoman   a cobbler   a clerk
a man so old he surely remembers other wars
an accordionist with a mendicant's cap
two squabbling children chalking hopscotch squares
with borrowed tailor's chalk
a shadowy figure crafting graffiti like calligraphy
walk-off parts in a film that's been made before

and *cut*

to the next scene
the Foley team already orchestrating sound
with metal sheets   tins of stones   real moans

the dead are no longer in frame
aftermath makes us all squeamish

so scatter their parts on the cutting room floor

the man with the wrong skin   the bossy little boy who might grow up to lead
the woman whose belly might birth an enemy   the teenager in his first yarmulke

*cut   splice   repeat*

keep the couple – we all love a wartime romance

## Zone
*after Irina Mashinski*


a week or so before the year pivots
        & December closes, like a coffin lid,
over the unnourished land;
        & hush now, here come
the bootless, the shoeless, the buttonless,
        curling their bony blue toes
over ice, spread like a punched-in
        windscreen over the wide fields;
beyond the treeline is the Border,
        gorgeous where the plum-dark sky
sinks below the earth's ooze;
        there is nothing here
you will recognise, not even this silver birch
        hanging like a smashed limb;
here's a rusting bike wheel, the torn canopy
        of a fragile and long-ago plane –
others have tried this –
        mud on their soles, their eyelids,
arms outstretched as if a loved one
        were waiting, casting a short, cold
shadow across the shifting Border;
        the moon rises, a brief howl of light,
before clouds trawl a darkness deeper
        than the childhood wells we drank from.

## Margot Fonteyn, 1944

*after a photograph by Lee Miller*

Sporting a high-rise fez-cum-Cossack combo filigreed with cascading star-petalled flowers. Her face, chiaroscuroed into expressionist angst on one side, clear and seer-eyed on the other. Her narrow shoulders sag with the weight of what she imagines – her father, thin as beaten tin, shackled in a POW camp. Each night she leaps higher and higher across the stage – *for you, for you* she whispers, flying from the wings.

## Mother Russia

adjusts her pillowy folds
she suspects they are no longer
enough to keep her little ones
from straying

she dances shadowy visions
of home across her whiteness
*hopeful hopeful*

        rosy-cheeked matryoshkas
        symphonies and sleigh-rides
        pickles and propaganda

but still they strain on the tips
of their fine toes
deciphering the beguiling codes
of western winds

they pull on seven-league boots
rehearse audacious leaps
across continents

she watches them
her nimble fledglings
tears freezing across her eyeballs
like curtains

      *Your Russian hearts will break*
      *Oh my Natasha  Rudi  Sasha  Mischa*

# Body Count

i.

Marlene wakes to Hollywood sunlight, brash on her Teutonic flesh, flesh she is ready to shed to gain cheekbones, lose her hausfrau sturdiness. Underneath she is the sleekest siren of stage and screen. She stretches like a never-ending cat, teeters on legs insured for so much they no longer feel part of her, as if, like Andersen's mermaid, she has borrowed their creamed and nyloned perfection. Yes, surely one day she will wake and once again be covered in scales, smoky vowels all undone.

ii.

Across an ocean, a bony Jewish boy folds himself into the biggest small space his family can afford. They have pulled gold from their teeth, fur from their backs for this boy, this boy who is a whole constellation of unsuitable stars. *Smaller than the boot of a Trabant,* he will tell his future lover, *my bones flat as a rat's, unmarrowed.*

iii.

Across the decades, the jigsaw of the world shifts. A girl sews. It's hard to push the blunt needle through the bright orange, though her thumbs are hard as hooves. She stuffs padding into the deep pockets. *Life vest.* She mouths the strange words, landlocked in her tight, sweating shack. Imagines hundreds of bodies floating, glowing like angels on a picture-book sea.

# Triangulation
*after Maria Stepanova*

### i.     Contamination

*the postbag snagged in the stream*
            like Stalker's dream
            facedown among the ripples
            with abandoned weaponry, bent icons
            Our Virgin Mother rusting from the eyes outwards

*the tin spoon*
*the quickstreams slipping the quicksilver*
            *slipsliding away[...]*
                        *and the narrow waters already round his knees*

Stalker's daughter moves the world with her mind

            *sing to me of how*

her radioactive legs are disobedient
            she is a shoulder-sitter   pick-a-back   piggy-back rider

\*\*\*

Come, Stalker will lead you to a Wonderland where scientists
find their hearts' desires ticking like death-watch beetles

ii.      **Famine**

*divested of alphabet…the greedy tongue […] writes in curds*

Come, come my little witch
do not break the only things we have
oh, how can your little mouth eat so much
  this bread hard as birch-wood,
        wetted and swallowed by your gummy mouth

                    *hush a bye baby*
                        *rocked and broken*
                            *on the treetops*
                                *down down baby*
                                    *cradle and all*

iii.      **Behind the Camera**

Tarkovsky stands at the edge of the world
              killer spores prick at the gates of his lips
              write an epitaph on his lungs

              the ground quivers

                    not yet   not yet   not yet

*Italics from Maria Stepanova's 'War of the Beasts and the Animals' (trans. Sasha Dugdale).*

*The post-apocalyptic landscape of 'Stalker' (Tarkovsky 1979) was filmed in a location heavily contaminated by industrial waste. The lengthy shooting schedule there significantly contributed to Tarkovsky's and other crew members' deaths. This prophetic film seems inspired by the Chernobyl disaster, but in fact predates it by seven years.*

## Scapegoat

A witch walks in a forest
        dank and deep as famine ache
where children are left to die
        like kittens in a sack.

The forest has many ways
        some straight   some narrow   some false –
of mud-slick   leaf-crush   pebbles   breadcrumbs.

A witch walks in a forest
        where a girl might step from the path
to squeeze juice from nettles
        ooze from mistletoe and chew chokeberries
with her long yellow teeth.

The forest has sealed itself in
        canopy heavy as a coffin lid
away from raven caw and thunder voice
        frostcrack and lightning bite.

A witch walks in a forest dragging dark tatters
        reaches its dense briared belly
hears the beat of old hearts –
        beech   oak   hawthorn.

This is where the stories are
        scavenged from dark thorn-held visions –
an abundance of rings   a worn red shoe
        a rolling crimson apple   one throat-shaped bite
taken from its flesh.

This is where rumours are birthed
        and rise like woodsmoke
whispering of plague   difference   fear.

A witch walks in a forest
　　　　sips her own spiced saliva
knows how each nest　burrow　den
　　　　holds its particular dormant alchemy.

A witch walks in a forest
　　　　not-woman　not-wife　not-daughter
she shapeshifts – tries feather　hide　fur
　　　　settles on goat　eyes like slit topaz –
stakes herself to the forest floor.

## Taken

Blood in the water, blood on the grass, shocking as the suffused sky, blue just moments before. Put down your gutting knife, your shoddily weighted priest, kneel before your night-kill, ask for the heart.

With eyes that find the inner shadow of things, their gathering mass, like closed fists, and the way they blink when we do not.

Remember when girls had nightdress cases in the shape of benign, familiar beings, maybe a teddy bear. Or some meaningless frilliness. Wonder at aunts like bad fairies offering their nieces nightmare cases on their thirteenth birthdays as they turn on that uncertain cusp, the witching day.

As the sun rose we took the path of the beast. It smelt of singe and was packed with a deep despair.

After we disappeared it was said Methodism made the most headway among the poor and the corn grew back so tall and fine that we became trapped in a pathless land, lurking low like pike amongst the hollow reeds.

## Blade

I am what I am, an untranslatable sharpness,
single-minded, sanguinary.
I can be blunted by the simple insertion
of a flat French vowel – *balade, balader* –
a stroll down slate-grey streets.
I am grass, shiny, whistling between your cupped hands.
Perhaps I'm a song crooned by curly-headed men,
or a tangy burst of anger
*cholemy! krwawy… kurewski…*
My truth is pallid, stretching over acres
of smouldering drought. I am vampire, superhero.
I am unsullied by diacritics,
the curled lip of an *ogonek,* the shrug of the *kreska.*
I am under your skin, your dancer's stance.
I can balance on thin ice, shave its smoothness
into hieroglyphics, cutting edge.
I could be youth, in a Regency coat, dashing.
I am the part of lips, the thrust of tongue
against your teeth, a smile before a half stutter.
      Say me.

## Interlude in a Locked Room
*after Yehuda Amichai*


The room's restraint, silent
as an empty glass, is the answer
to a forgotten question.

A flag unwinds in the clattering wind,
long as a shroud, wide as a veil.
Fields smoulder in the distance

sometimes there is a truncated cry.
The air in the room is squat and old,
too ugly to breathe.

The dust tastes bitter, like ancient lemons,
reshaping itself as if a cat had just left
a patch of sunlight.

A row of old shoes, full
of sweat and air; a windowsill smeared
with fingerprints, witness to nothing
that can easily be recalled.

## The Distractor Brides of St Petersburg

Slowly we realise that at every corner
the same scene is unfolding:
a glossy white stretch limo,
entwined gold rings on the sleek bonnet,
blonde or brunette bee-hived brides
in creamy satin and thick white pelts.

Classic vistas frame their radiance:
the Birzhevoy Bridge, the River Neva
freezing to a still, grey porridge.
The Winter Palace, St Isaac's Cathedral,
the Saviour on Spilled Blood's patterned domes
turning snowflakes into kaleidoscopes.

Fairy-tale scenes of Snow Queenliness,
mosaics of smashed champagne flutes,
icy streams of celebration,
floating feathers of released doves.
We stop once, twice, ten times –
uninvited witnesses of breathless promises
hanging in the air like frozen banners.

As we watch, the silky fingers of Petersburg
pickpockets expertly take all we have.
By the time we realise all the brides are identical,
with their fixed matryoshka smiles,
we are naked from head to toe.

We stumble down Nevsky Prospect towards our hotel
along a conveyor belt of rolling champagne bottles,
our pink skin hoaring, ice at our hearts and groins.

## Concert on the Herzbaracke Cabaret Boat, Lake Zurich

The chill of a milky blue day evaporates
in the womb of the cabaret boat.
We sit on baroque-backed seats
crinolined girls serve champagne
Piaf crackles her tales of *la vie en rose*
a silver-haired woman at the next table
unwraps a string of shrouded stars.

Time passes – rust thickens, a leaf changes
from red to russet –
the curtains part:
a klezmer band darns the threads
of a murdered past
with songs from the shtetl, clarinet calls,
the mournful underlinings of a double-bass,
the unbroken fingers of the pianist.

**II**

## Royal Academy of Dancing 1981

Autumn, and the sun's tearing through the London grey.
I'm in the office, the coffee's on, the blur
of comings and goings has begun; there are fifty people
in this building and I know all of them by name.
I'm nineteen, mind full of sex and fun and dance,
trying to secure the golf ball on my typewriter
so it doesn't break free when the letters whirr.
Someone's pliéing in the kitchen while the kettle boils;
overhead the dancers jeté to a piano on repeat;
the corridors smell of rosin, sweaty practice clothes, feet.
My big glass ashtray's choked with Camels, Marlboros,
scavenged Rothmans, paperclips.
Through the window I see my blue bike in the cobbled yard,
locked and leaning; my boss's Morgan nosing through the gates,
yellow as the tulips one of the heartbroken summer boys
(cheekbones like Rudi, eyes like Baryshnikov) gave me in July
the day after I tended his blistered, bleeding feet.
There are Dames on every floor, gliding to the studios,
veiled in hairspray, Parma violets, Chanel.
The girls mouth *madame* then it's feet on the barre
and pain to the rhythm of an ivory tipped cane.
Tempers are rising from the ground floor up, the lift pings;
I ignore the accusing filing cabinet, the exams to translate,
the accounts to tabulate, the Gestetner that makes me high,
the telexes to send to other hemispheres, and go walkabout,
check everyone's still there, in their rightful place.
The disease is here but we don't know it: no-one's missing yet.
I line everyone up, like an old school photograph,
turn my back for a minute and half of them are gone.

# I have made coffee for the women who danced for Diaghilev

taken the minutes of the committee meetings of their lives
shorthand flying across the page like the Russian endearments he would use
to make them blush pink as their layers of grubby on-tour tulle;

I have served their coffee on the Adeline Genée table, buffed by decades
of elegant elbows, where they gossip like girls, arthritic fingers fluttering
with invitations to the dance, eternal puppet-master with his *Petrushka* dolls –
they whisper *Sergei Sergei* when they think I'm not listening;

I have refilled their cups as they beat time, time, time with their maestra canes
admired their perfect posture, their hair piled as if to hold a tiara in place
through 32 fouettés spun until their eyes and hearts bulge;

I have washed their fragile cups as I picture him in that thick greatcoat
with the furred collar, a homburged Russian gangster.
Did he have a heart under all that? Only a broken one.
*Nijinksy, crazed and beloved faun.*

They pick up their shawls and sticks and rise on misshapen toes
still ready to answer his Svengali call.

## Cento – Nureyev
*after John Percival*


his parents were both Tartars
a lonely child
Nureyev danced 9 times as the Prince
his beloved teacher Pushkin
virtually under house arrest
Nureyev was warned
he kept out of sight behind a pillar
the ballerinas were in tears
people knew he was around
he breathed to blur the image
developed to a high pitch
whipped into movement
the soaring quality lithe springiness
long high grands jetés
he appeared to hover in the air
left his mark indelibly
the fire of his personality
the brightness of the light thrown

## Taboo

*he died after a long and serious illness*
not because of a four-letter word,
a word as meaningless as half
a sticking plaster or
the plural of help that never came;
an acronym turned inside out
in France and Spain where
its sound is a majestic tree
of incorruptibility, eternal life,
secret host to honey fungus,
aphid attack.

> Four letters, one syllable,
> lips rictus-stretched,
> a final hissing sibilant,
> the unwilling tongue cradled
> by teeth.

The smallest container for such enormity –
like cupped hands with the world pouring through.

*AIDS – Acquired Immune Deficiency Syndrome. I was living in Paris when Bryce died.*
*The French acronym for AIDS is SIDA which is pronounced like 'cedar'...*

## Confetti Dancers

The boys, the boys, the beautiful boys
they flirt in the dark like courtesans,

flex their impossible, satined feet
cast their perfect silhouettes
slender shadow puppets;

the boys, the boys, the beautiful boys
leaping and turning like swirled confetti
barrelling across the stage
faster than a blink –
jeté, fouetté, cabriole

the boys, the boys, the beautiful boys
all in a line to take their bows
smiles bright in the spotlight

until tomorrow guns them down
and we're clapping an empty stage
sobbing *Bravo! Bravo!*
to the echoing wings.

## Last Supper

I didn't know I was saying goodbye, just
that there was a different quality to the way
you hugged me.

The four of us laughing round the rickety table:
Martin, shadowy, quiet, your rock, your backdrop.

Terry, older, courtly. I remember the day
he bought my bike, he'd heard how poor I was,
even though the saddle barely reached his knee.

And you, pulling your sleeves over the blotches
dancing down your arms, a livid notation.

Maybe we gossiped – the latest scandals
bourréeing across the table; maybe we ate fish;
maybe we laughed at Terry, camping it up.

I only remember what we didn't talk about,
that silent assassin that took you all.

# Positions

### first position

*more powerful // than God*

### second position

*hard to talk about //          // a big rotting log*

### third position

*do not be afraid //*
*each has a story to tell*

### fourth position closed

*plaguepandemicvirusjudgement //*
*weakeningisolatebestworst*

### fourth position open

*suppress the co-factors*
*//*
*provide safe harbour*

### fifth position

*a virus with no morality //*
*stories of blood and trust*


*This poem uses text from websites referring to AIDS/HIV.*

## In Heaven

On Rue du Pont Neuf two guys are taking a selfie,
      backs to the rococo swirls of the Louis Vuitton entrance.

They look so well, so happy, and I wonder if you and M
      would be like this, if you'd lived.

The sky's a vicious blue today; I imagine you both up there
      hosting outrageous parties,

fancy dress compulsory, scrawling **"no angels"** on the invites,
      copyrighting dance moves with Freddie and Rudi

under the pumping light of the stars;
      looking down on our dramas – rolling your eyes…

      There's so much I want to tell you,
*I wrote a poem about you; it got published; I hope you don't mind…*

      You're already laughing at my Englishness,
Australian vowels wider than ever, *Naaaah!*

      *I'm still married,* I say, *can you believe it? We've been together
      for longer than you've been dead.*

A man hurries past, frowning;
      it's not every day you see a woman talking to herself without a phone.
*It's considered a sign of genius,* I mutter, high-fiving a passing cloud.

### Obituary for your last pair of ballet shoes

Let's start here, at the end
        how we cradle them heel to toe
in fifth position
        into a cardboard box
as gently as if they were hamsters, guinea pigs
        or a very small rabbit
only the airholes are missing.

Let's go back to the last day you wore them
        no, let's not
let's go back to the days of those leaps
        higher than cliff falls, heartstopping
the days when you wore out so many pairs
        they would fill a foreign field.

Let's bury these, scarred with twist, stretch and spring,
        at the bottom of this trunk
no, let's not
        let's put them here on this high shelf
by an open window
        where the fast blink of our tears
creates an illusory flickerbook of flight.

## My boss is a sculpture by Enzo Plazzotta

you are a leap of bronze, scanning the Thames from your pedestal,
muscled as a Michelangelo. Below is an old red phone box steeped
in the reek of metal and urine; a phone book, pages Bible-thin, for
terpsichorean emergencies;

cast in flight a decade before you swapped dance shoes for
dictaphone, for paperclip, for fax. I would see you point and flex
and stretch behind your yawning desk, waiting all day for the curtain
to fall.

## Dead Friend as Imaginary Dog

You've lived longer in my mind
than in the flesh; less tangible
than that scratchy make-believe cat
I used to blame for everything

when my soundscape was the chittering
white noise typical of onelings –
like today's lone walkers on the beach
who gossip to their loll-tongued dogs.

It's called bemagination, this fuzzy line
between belief and imagination.
In another century you would be
household god, familiar, guardian angel.

So, my darling, I bemagine you as greyhound:
ribby dancer's torso, burdened eyes,
prim toenails. By my side. Ready to listen.

## Praise Song for the Plié

for five crazed Twister feet positions
for slowmo quad-burn squat
& stomach-clench pull-up
for butterfly wing turnout
for muscle-binding all in one low flow
for Pavlova, Nijinsky, Baryshnikov,
   Fonteyn, Aldous, Cragun
for Danilova's pretty knees
for Rudi in holey woolly triple-layers
guarding his sinews like ropes of gold
for vodka's loosening anaesthetic hit
for the demi-plié – semi-wince morning curtsy to the night before
for sneeze-smell memory of rosin and sweat
for arm swoop Royal Ballet fingers
for the backstage Degas poster-girl pose
for the chair-back, windowsill, worktop, bus stop
for the Charlie Chaplin stance at the kitchen sink
for the never-ending Tchaikovsky earworm
for my good straight back
thank you

# Interlude

## Read Their Lips

*in response to the 1916 documentary film "Battle of the Somme" shot on location
by Geoffrey Malins and John McDowell*

This story has been told before:
how the trees stood in dark rows, like widows,

how birdsong left the land, save for the calls
of urgent owls, bright in the mute darkness.

How the moon climbed to uncharted heights
to flee the reek of brimstone.

How poppies slumbered for a hundred years
waiting for the world to change.

How the villagers returned, one by one,
carrying their hurt in their pockets.

How they laid their cheeks against
the fissured land, salted it.

And how, in the nearness of now,
the sons and daughters of the sons and daughters

of the sons and daughters come
wearing flowers like pilgrim badges.

How they pluck at the past,
how it runs through their fingers

like hourglass sand, how they
raise their faces to the darkening sky,

mouth their tales, individual, endless
as the passing flakes of snow.

Cut.

See this man, so familiar
he could be my father's
grandfather,
see how he strolls
in this flickering parade
freak-show of the long dead,
these men, chalky as fairground prizes
with their virgin bandages
angling their smiles stage right
teeth worn to shadows,
resisting the flinch and itch
of lice squirming in the seams
of sweat-caked uniforms

dogs at their heels – a silent barking
coal in their pockets for luck

a trail of horses on the horizon
like a biblical caravan.

Read their lips:
*send my love to Ma and Doris and all my little ones*
*have a pint in the Crown on me Arthur, you lucky bugger…*

In her narrow Manchester bed
a woman dreams of her lover,
runs towards his muddy back
the distance between them undiminished
until, in a moment of stop-motion illogic,
she is touch-close,
rising on tiptoe
to kiss him
where his mouth used to be.

The camera tracks – left, right, left, right, left, right,
16 miles of grey fields, fissures like snow, smoke like cumuli
turning the July sun into January cladmurk

*Don't look back.*

Off frame there's a technicolour world
a behind-the-scenes kaleidoscope of bleed and heave
a blink away
over the mute horizon a crater of sound
Bosch jigsaw of body-parts cupped in a stinking crucible, cordite forged

Cut.

I watch you watching the film for the first time
eyeballs palpitating to the turns of a hand-cranked camera
processing your own ghostly flicker-book
1, 2     1, 2     1, 2, 3, 4     1, 2, 3, 4, 5, 6, 7, 8

Cut.

*Intertitle:*
*Industrious Peasants Continue Their Activities Just Outside the Firing Line*
Two women,
poke-bonneted, sturdy as blinkered warhorses,
clothed as if Van Gogh hadn't died nearly thirty years before.
Gleaning, or perhaps they are planting dragon's teeth,
hoping to harvest the next crop of young men,
fully grown, fully armed by the first of July.
This is all they have, this precarious field,
this tilted horizon.

Cut.

The camera pans…

Back to these endless lines of marching men
arm in arm for all time, for auld lang syne,
singing *A Long Way to Tipperary*
as if it's not a cliché.
Sure of who they are – sound of limb,
dog-tags still with their rightful owners.
Soon they will rise to become *The Missing of the Somme*,
faith broken on the hard-rimmed wheel of war,
ghosting the sky like a new constellation
whispering *inconnu inconnu inconnu*

**III**

# Emily

My grandmother is a secret
protected from my father's dislike
by my mother's silence.

She died when I was four;
lives on in the redness
of my mother's hair
and songs from the music-halls,
recalled in her smoker's croak.

Here she is on her wedding day.
See how her veiled fragility
balances on white satin heels;
how she surrenders
to the iron grip
of my gangster-suited grandfather.

# Cuckoo Sister

An hour ago she heard the aunts
clustered like good fairies
round her new sister's pram
in the afternoon sun:

> *she's so sweet, so pretty*
> *her eyes are so bright*
> *she's so good and quiet*

Now she sits in the dark
on a horsehair pouffe
that smells of nervousness

wondering how babies die.
She remembers the neighbour's child,
blue-lipped in its tiny shroud.

The next morning she prays
so hard and long
her knees are scored
with the hassock's grain.

She breathes the Sunday smell
of incense and polish –
wonders if God
will ever speak to her again.

## Down Under

It was all she knew, or all I remember, eavesdropping under the blue Formica table where most of childhood took place, fenced in by the nyloned legs of aunts.

*After the murder, he escaped to Australia down a manhole cover.*

If I unfurl the scroll of my mother's East End family tree, farfetched as a Gothic novel, I'll find Great Uncle Pat, *missing, believed dead.*

Here he is, crawling through sewers, down, down, fighting rats for scraps, clothes thinning, humming Nana Em's music-hall songs for sanity, brain so cobwebbed with fear he hears echoing footsteps however deep he goes, every shadow a noose, until he emerges, naked, blinded, into sunlight, to be greeted by Skippy, the Bush Kangaroo. As the sun sets he sits by a perfect campfire, sings *Waltzing Matilda* in the voice of Rolf Harris.

This is all I know.

## Boxes

*Your granddad brought them back for me,*
tight Sunderland vowels raised
over the care home clatter.

Blue and cream, German folk art,
they smell of hand-cream, cold metal.
I wonder at the love in this,
remember how her face powder
covered her sadness.

I picture him in stained khaki
reeking of piss and Riesling
picking through the bones
of a Berlin street, looting boxes
for his wife, tarnished trinkets
for his girlfriends.

Another box, wedged at the back
of a hideous tallboy,
rough-carved rosewood, edged
in petal-thin ivory.
*From my missionary lover*
*before me and your Grandad met*
*at the VE-Day Dance at the Empire.*

I think of her, maid's uniform
unfolding in his holy embrace,
her face, unpowdered, bright.

## Kingston 1965-1979

Brady's arcade – down-on-their-luck dealers with blackened coins,
ribbonless medals, smelly stamps, things that look just dug;
coffee beans roasting in the Apple Market's smeary café;
Woolworths – cover version hits, Pic 'n' mix;
Tommy Steele singing *'Alf a Sixpence* in the warm worn plush
                                                    of the Granada;
C & A; Green Shield Stamps – their dizzy lick;
walking barefoot to Hampton Court Palace like it's the summer of love;
Queen Anne, gilded and stout on her plinth by the Guildhall;
the Coronation Stone where I conjure Saxons perched in full regalia;
Richmond Park – hollow trees, the understanding eyes of deer;
the Thames, my primeval soup, coursing strong and dirty in my veins,
how one way led to the hammering boatyards where dad was king,
the other to London, punk, Harold Wilson;
how it took a sharp left turn, became the narrow Hogsmill
flowing past my street and all the boys with dangerous eyes, flick-knives;
how once there was a cocoanut matting mill, here,
                          where the chip shop belches its oily breath
towards our little house with its secret well, hairy walls,
                          my unloved dolls, your futile Lego.

# The Child in Me [...]
*after Fernando Pessoa*


still watches shadows on walls
a cast of characters
who've never lived but may have died

still summons the hive with bee vowels
joins their lavender thrum   *zdum zdum*
dances a ronde of parallels

still hides from the exposing glass
turns outside in and inside out
wrong smiles   uncertain feet

still sees how the rain lifts the earth
to show the lying root

### Don't tell anyone about the well

says dad –
I peer under the lid
expect to see the moon
shining back at me like a golden cake
instead I'm leaning into
an endless darkness

*ding dong bell* I whisper
and I know my childhood
is down there now
throwing my words
back at me in a ghostly game of catch.

Over the years I watch dad strip
the warm guts from rooms –
the hearths and tiles,
the ancient copper in the corner,
the pantry, the red floor that bled
when it was mopped.
Soon cottage became extension
became house.

At school my best friend
grips my hand, shouts
*Riminy Rominy Ro!*
*And it's down the well we go!*
We jump, smack!
onto the playground tarmac
squatting and weaving our bodies
and arms as if falling through the air.

I'm not allowed to tell her about the sinkhole
below the clean white shell
of our new lounge,
the kind of shell you lift to your ear
and it tells you of nothing.

I can't say I don't like her new game,
that she doesn't know what having a well
in your life is really like – for she is a real girl
and I am just thin meniscus
terrified of breaking.

At night I sit
listening to the electric fire creak
as it cools and re-heats.
Alone on the Ercol sideboard,
glowing, is a bowl,
an almost perfect globe,
amber glass punctuated with bubbles
like the final exhalations
of trapped insects.

I fidget and twitch,
invading my parents' nightly game of statues.
They turn, brand me
with yet another imagined illness
*St Vitus Dance, like your sister*
hisses mum to dad.

I can never ask the question
my restlessness covers
*dad, before you built us over the well,*
*did you fill it in?*

## Russian Doll

See how she fits in the palm of your hand –
shiny, saffron, crimson, her painted smile;

break her apart into seven versions of self,
see how her features falter as she shrinks,

her smile a brush-flick, an afterthought,
the kind of girl you could easily lose

down the side of a sofa.
See how well her layers are concealed,

she looks complete, how could you guess
what's inside, where the joins are?

See how hard she has tried to resist
the attempts to align repeating patterns;

how she has always insisted on being off-kilter
by a millimetre, a fraction, a lifetime.

## My mother was

                    a Christmas tree
shedding needles in sharp piles the carpet
could not release

                    a snowglobe
teetering under an unstable sky, lip-reading
our reluctant greetings

                    the false shine
of baubles, tinsel, the hard glitter
of unwanted cards

                    cold turkey
on Boxing Day, an obstinate morsel
gristled to carcass

                    the way
Christmas would end before it had begun –
a broken toy at day's end

# The Tutu in my Wardrobe

crowds unworn dresses
into mothy corners
        remembers the days
my mother hoped for a girl
to mould into her unlikeness

it will not let me lift it out
        test its stiff defiance
instead unfurls into hissing swan
recalling when I would wave my arms
a tiny tree in a thin leotard

the tutu in my wardrobe
yellows and brittles
tells me I already know the answer
to the question
that breaks the spell

the tutu is kin to my mother's wedding veil
sometimes I would try this on
pushing a new hole through the cheap lace
that tried to hold us all – a keepnet.

## Restoration

The floor has been mopped,
the jug turned on its head to drain
next to a glass, cloudy, old, its scratches
a lightly etched landscape.

There is a quietness over the Formica,
the carefully wiped surfaces,
the unturned knob of the cooker.

The front door is still open wide
to let the sunshine in, the drama out.
My bare feet find a pill you dropped
near the orange plastic pedal bin.

I flush it down the sink with the others,
put the bottle back on the highest shelf,
the tremble in my hand echoing yours
just moments before.

## Laundry Marks

The half-remembered days of sunlight, rain,
sheets laid out to dry like homespun shrouds.

Those honeymoon days in India, the taste of fenugreek,
silks in bright earth colours, humid, limp;

a dead body, my first, loosely wrapped,
garlanded with marigolds, ash on the breeze.

Our clothes, soiled with sweat-stains like maps,
disappear for days then find us, blank

again, colour-coded in silken threads
that may have said *the one with ghost hair*

or *the girl with uneven eyes* for all we knew.
I think of dad pairing mum's thin socks,

their different ribs and turns of heel –
her failing eyes, fingers bent like commas,

her toes fighting downwards, downwards
towards the certain knowledge of cul-de-sac.

# Today there was a cliffslide

and I have made a list of the words I don't want to talk about/the first item is two words *stomach* + *pump*/I'm not going to talk about how old I was/when I first heard these words/what I believed they meant/how they seeped into everything like slow damp/instead I'm going to talk about the books I was reading/*Jill and the Perfect Pony*/how I became Jill/flying through woods and air and applause until my hacking jacket glowed with rosettes – red red and more red/blue blue blue/yellow yellow yellow/*The Lion, The Witch and The Wardrobe* and how I had such a place/hung with nana's furs pungent as bear/how here I *was* Lucy/chosen child/queen of another land/Lucy/who didn't seem to mind/the theft of her childhood/

the second word on the list is *section*/I want to point out that this is a transitive verb/but it's also a noun meaning a part/a division/a fraction/find a formula for the following: if an unwanted child discovers the rules of abortion/how long will it take her to unbirth herself/

the third word on the list is *celebration*/because we didn't/I'm not going to talk about how what should have been a bracelet full of shiny charms/is just a dull, empty chain/how I still wait for the promised meal in a 70s Chinese restaurant/the gloop of monosodium glutamate/the tacky carmine of spare ribs/

it was good not to talk about all these things/there are many more words I don't want to talk about/but for now I'm going to slip this list between the muddy clumps of cliffslide/one day a girl like me will find it/maybe she will unsay it into a new language/and she will believe it is a praise-song from another world/

## Mother, folded small

Your mother flaunted her death wish like the blowsy corsage pinned to her pretty coats. Your father gave up his river life the day he pulled a woman from the Thames, hair bright in the water like a distress flare.

Once you found your mother's doppelganger in a magazine. Straight red hair. Green eyes. Long pale face. But smiling. After your mother tore through the family albums like an iconoclast you carried false mother with you always. Folded small.

Sometimes your mother would tease you by pricking her thumbs bloody with the long pin of her corsage. On those days the pill bottles would be in a different order. Emptier. Their brown sides translucent in the bathroom light.

In the end, she was not the one who chose.

She left you her corsage, pulsating like a butterfly in your unwilling hands. *Go back,* you chant. *Go back to chrysalis… to caterpillar…to tiny egg. Let me grind you under my sure heel.*

# Lament

When they lift you
we see the small miracle of the bedsheet
imprinted with your dark sweat.

You have found a path to the past
calling *Mum!* to the grandmother
I never knew.

The flat-line lives up to expectations
the one-note drone of television drama
a few random spikes
the stillness punctured by the woman
in the corner bed who implores *Karen!*
every time I pass as if she has guessed
my forgotten middle name.

On the way home, straddling the path
there's a collared dove's wingspan,
braced with a bloodied breastbone.
I fix on the sparrow-hawk's butchery,
dull the memory of the cancer's
slow, satisfied feeding.

A homeless man on all fours smokes, entranced,
into the shadow his face casts.
I crouch, offer him coins for his eyes.

# Dream-walking

not-yet-woman   no-longer-girl
I am walking towards the park
bare feet filthy from the pavement's bite
I am hippy-me
cheesecloth shirt   a cousin's castoff
jeans long enough to grow into
wrists braceleted with leather thongs

in my bag
the poems of Rupert Brooke
two slices of Mother's Pride
a tiny jar of gritty fish-paste
pocket money to buy
the only Italian hot chocolate in Surrey

in my pocket
a red-haired woman
a wound
the smell of sawdust

royal deer run here
to a soundtrack of Bolan & Bowie

I recite sonnets to the dog-peed   heel-scrunched grass

stag beetles tumble from branches like blackened conkers
a thunderous crack as a falling oak buries my shadow
bruises on my arm –
five perfect purple screams

somewhere there's a hidden river

but I don't want to hear its awkward questions
its weed-choked voice

# Coda

## In the Museum of Tiny Epiphanies [Catalogue Extracts]

First word –

>            not *mama* or *dada*
>            probably a thirteen-month old version of
>                        *you must be joking*

From the catalogue –

>            Dad tells me –
>                        *we were on a boat   you were three*
>                                    *I was steering*
>                        *I kept telling your mum*
>                                    *'you need to keep an eye on her'*
>                        *but she just gave me the flat eye*
>                                    *and I thought*
>                        *'she wouldn't care if you drowned'*

First memory –

>            sitting high in my kitchen sink bath
>                        covered in crazy foam
>                        water tepid   scummy
>                        mum sitting in a chair
>                        limp as milk
>                        life unspooling in her head

Centrepiece –

>                        high and dry on the West Bank
>                        my Israeli lover shows me
>                        his machine-gun
>                        this is not a cliché
>
>                        it is not my cowboy-mad cousins
>                        trying to John Wayne walk
>                        or water-pistols in brittle reds
>                        and yellows like boiled sweets

this is a hard dark thing
and inside are bullets
with my name on

I tell him the safety's off

*these could be my last words*
at the last second
he swings away
from the dotted line leading
to my holding-its-breath heart
kills the wall instead
my clothes
still strewn on the bed
post coital
peppered with smouldering holes


this still feels like something I dreamt

Last memory –


how the sea is like baptism
so cold at first nothing gets through
then sensation knife-like
hundreds of icy paper cuts
the little mermaid
receiving her legs
learning what *human* means

## White Nights

there are nights when I count the silence between owls    when a
muntjac's drama queen scream is midnight's backdrop    when the
stars' glow mocks the dull gleam of a cooling kettle    & it's both
too late & too early for tea    there are nights when I    rustle    clink
pad    whimper    an insomniac's soundtrack muffled as if by the
grace of snowfall    nights when I conjure the warm sprawl of a cat
I've never owned    when being awake feels like being dead    *dear
smallest hour*    where my tiniest thoughts become the tread of giants

## Desire Lines

A child stands, mouth a cartoon O of disbelief,
blood drips from her hands. She has cupped

a spiny fish like a chalice across a shiny lake.
Behind her fishermen mock like the upside down

men in a tarot pack. Maybe this is the day
she understands the world is not a toyshop

open all hours, just for her. Her palms sting
like rope burns as they heal.

A decade later, winter again. Centre stage –
a samovar, misting the room like dry ice.

The girl's mother takes her hand, traces
her future in the scars, says:

*I see two men. One is driving down a dark road,*
*lost, in a tiny car.*

*The other is standing on a Dutch boat, searching*
*the sea with salt-struck eyes.*

*Avoid them both.*

*Seek instead a boy who once fished for minnows.*
*He will show you a travelling man who conjures poets*

*from his pockets like doves, scatters their songs*
*as far as he can reach. Together you will seek*
*the silence before it all began.*

## Healing

This morning, such a sunrise –
we stand, naked, complicit,

watching its deep & murderous red.
After, your long bones spoon my belly

& we drift in & out of early birdsong.
I tap the morse of everything unsaid

down the warmth of your sleeping back.
Sometimes I want to lick you into shape,

just-born, the living shock of your salt.
There were days when we had no energy

to kiss – your cough edging into every breath,
the idea of *us* scarifying, a slow erasure

with each letter's drone:
*another date, another test, another wait.*

You keep a secret diary bound in sallow plastic,
I suture my grief with long, messy lines,

consider dying my hair amethyst to match
the half-moon testaments to the nights

I dream you into peripheral vision –
reimagine other lives, litanies of *what-ifs.*

But now here we are, or here you are –
secure in the miracle of more.

## Snowdream

This year we have all learnt
what it means to be snowed in,
to have drunk our fill of its burn.

Some mornings I sing the snow to life,
populate my garden with imagined snowmen –
dark-eyed, top-hatted – their long embrace
my only source of warmth.

I only know three words for snow:
     *slow   quiet   cold*

Once there was a man who died
planting his flag in a vast white wildness,
his name the echo of a high-wheeling bird
that dives for small, unburied things –
Falcon to my blazing Snow Queen.

# #stayathome

You dream you are a saint again, always joining the story late, eschewing the long haul of goodness, fast-forwarding to the great demise. You can never see yourself, dreams don't work like that. You are behind the camera, directing the vast cast of your legend, learning the manner of your death by the burning reflection on their retinas.

You'll rise, as usual, dust the skirting boards, hummus for lunch, a few more pages of Hilary Mantel, survive the rabbit-in-the-headlights viewing of *News at Ten*.

And in the small hours, you'll slip unseen into a widescreen epic where you'll be martyred once more on sunlit streets and open fields by invisible and myriad forces.

## Glow

Alexanders are legion in the hedgerow, girding this shrunken world with lime-green early sweetness; broken stalks leak tangy sap – Roman celery. Their lacy heads start to seed and spike. Dandelion heads, thistles – shapes that hook and stick – evoke invisible enemies – magnified on every screen. Somewhere an artist has cast the particle in glass, two million times actual size – femme fatale of the virus world.

Let's rethink this. Look, the seed-heads are like clusters of stars. Gaze upwards – the generosity of the bright night sky will show us how to navigate this fearful newness.

LIVE CANON